"Can't Nobody Take Me Away!"

"Can't Nobody Take Me Away!"

Written By:

Kyran M. Daisy

Cover design, graphic design: Designs by…Kyran

1stBooks rev. 11/29/00

ABOUT THE BOOK

Can't Nobody Take Me Away! is a wonderful journey into the mind of a writer who is blossoming into the full power of creative expression. Presented in lyric verse, the body of work is deeply moving and emotional, expressing a wide variety of emotions and social commentary. Deeply introspective and ambient, the author creates a mood and sets a stage that will captivate the audience's senses and transport them to another place and time.

The embodiment of four years of writing, *Can't Nobody Take Me Away!* is a telling tale of the author's growth as a writer and a person. The title poem has earned several awards as well as publications and audio recordings. Confident, vulnerable, defiant, and endearing, this book is a testament to strength and fortitude showing that strength comes through vulnerability, honesty, and self-knowledge. The author stands in radiant defiance declaring: "I am here to stay" and I believe him.

DEDICATION

Dedicated with love
to my mother, my father,
my sister Nicole, and my grandmother.

TABLE OF CONTENTS

CAN'T NOBODY TAKE ME AWAY!

AFTER THE RAIN

CLOSER TO YOU

EYES OF A LOST SOUL

WHISPERS OF YOU

THE STORM

So I'll wait until the day the bell of freedom rings,

afraid to face the light for the pain that vision brings.

Praying love and compassion will soon be the norm,

but until then I live on the edge of the storm.

JUST ANOTHER DAY

He's all by himself,
The one over there
with the denim jacket
and greasy black hair.

There's a rumor about him,
He called me a name.
But, he didn't know
how to play my game.

The very next morning
his body's not found.
He's living in hiding
six feet underground.

I move to the corner
to make my next deal.
It's been years since my youth,
my savior was steel.

I move from the corner,
The time nine o'clock.
I enter a building,
just sold my last rock.

Those guys look suspicious.
What's this all about?
They're holding my number.
They're taking me out.

I'm shot in the back,
the killing unseen.
I'm too young to die,
I'm only fifteen.

They're friends of the punk
that I killed last night.
The smiles on their faces
my very last sight.

The sound of confusion
ringing in my ears.
I heard someone's scream
I felt someone's tears.

My body is moved,
someone by my side.
The sound of the school bell
ringing as I died.

WAR ZONE

You play with my mind
as if it's a game.
The people may change
but the story's the same.

A new generation.
The children are lost
Just trying to survive,
but look at the cost.

There are drugs on the corner,
guns in the schools.
With no education,
we're raising tough fools.

The gangs are all over
Ready to attack.
I can't turn a corner
without watching my back.

"I made it to lunch,
no one started a fight.
If I cut my last class,
I'll get home alright."

In the midst of such chaos,
you say that we're wild.
My body is young,
but I'm not a child.

I've been living in danger,
Watching my tracks,
I feel like I'm falling,
slipping through the cracks.

I keep changing myself,
but myself I remain.
It seems there's no way
of escaping my pain.

I look up and it's raining,
the raindrops, my tears.
I cry for my future.
I cry for my fears.

STREET LIFE

The streets are unsafe here
They kill and they rape.
And so many people
turn to drugs to escape

A world full of lies.
A world filled with deceit.
Everywhere that you turn
it's all that you'll meet.

Just look in my eyes,
they're red and they strain.
They mirror the truth
and echo my pain.

I'm born in a time
I was not meant to be.
There's no reason or rhyme
for what's happened to me.

Maybe it was my mother
who beat me for love
or my drunken father,
rest his soul up above.
Got to get away!
Got to get away!
Got to get away!
So I can face another day!

Trying something new
when the day is through,
nothing left to do...

NOT A CHILD

Just seven years old.
She'd known him so long.
She called him her uncle,
never thought he'd do wrong.

On the night of her birth,
he took center stage.
Promised her presents
as coming of age.

He took her upstairs.
The door was then locked
Her glee disappeared,
her pathway was blocked.

He gave her a kiss
She started to cry
He said "I won't hurt you."
He whispered that lie.

Her protests unvoiced,
her voice lost within.
She fell to the ground,
acquiesced to the sin.

And when they returned,
she withdrew from the scene
and took to the shadows
afraid and unclean.

She told no one of this,
Her secret was kept.
Her only escape
had come when she slept.

She cried in the day
She cried in the night
She prayed for her death
at morning's first light.

No longer a girl now,
though fragile and mild.
Her body is young,
but she's not a child.

I AM BUT ONE

I met an old man while shopping,
I tried to pass without stopping,
but as I passed by this man
he stretched out his hand
and turned to me and said:

"I stand before you humble and poor.
I've been 'round town begging door to door.
Find it in your heart to do a good deed
and help a fellow man in his time of need."
To which I replied:

"I am but one,
In number I'm few.
One's effort is futile,
How can I help you?"
and I went on my way.

I came across a woman begging with child.
Her clothing unkempt; hair matted and wild.
As I passed through the crowd, she called out to me.
Two others stopped also, making us three.
She turned to me and said:

"I stand before you and I'm just about due.
I've no shelter to stay in. I don't know what to do.
Look into your soul and see
if you can have some pity on me."
To which I replied:

"I am but one,
In number I'm few.
One's effort is futile,
How can I help you?"
and I turned away.

I saw a little boy further up the street.
"I stand before you tired and haggard.
My hunger's overwhelming, my walking is staggered.
You can see from my wrists that my bones have no meat.
Won't you please provide me with something to eat."
I thought to myself:

"I can feed him once, but what more can be done?
For in the end, you see, I am but one."
I turned to him and said:

"I am but one,
In number I'm few.
One's effort is futile
How can I help you?
and I continued on my way.

It is now quite a few years after that day.
I no longer ignore people in my usual way.
You see, my crops have all failed and my cattle are dead.
I've no place where I can rest my head.
In my wildest dreams I never thought it could be
that the next beggar I met turned out to be me.

"My crops have all failed, and my cattle have died."
Into a crowd of strangers I cried.
"You there! Please listen! And you!
Everything I tell you is true!
I've nothing to eat and I've no place to stay.
Please, help me in some small way."

With tears in my eyes I turned to face each
and one by one they echoed my speech.

AND STILL I DREAM

And still I dream,
I dream we'll rise above this hell,
reclaim our world
and use and taste it.
Where we're not judged by our outer shell.
Where our lives
are never wasted.

And still I dream,
I dream of racial harmony
and that we can live
this life together
I dream that love's a symphony
that fills our world
and reigns forever

And still I dream
our love will reach every mountain high
and ocean deep
and keep on flowing
until the last one of us dies
and they will keep
the gift of knowing.

HERALD THE DAY

Herald the day when truth and justice reign,
when love comes down like rain
and erases all of the pain.

Herald the day when beggars don't clutter the street,
when the starving have enough to eat,
and children don't die at our feet.

Herald the day when people start changing their ways,
when the sunlight is not blocked by haze,
and people don't die from its rays.

Herald the day when all people are thought of as pure:
minority, gay, or with aids,
and each disease possesses a cure.

Herald the day when judgment is not based on skin
when equality is not a sin,
and freedom finds its way in.

Herald the day when there is no longer war or sorrow,
when weapons aren't something to borrow,
and we look to a brighter tomorrow.

Herald the day when violence does not entertain,
when blood's not a typical stain,
and voices do not cry in vain.

CAN'T NOBODY TAKE ME AWAY!

You discriminate against me based on my skin,
but I knew that I'd finally find my way in.
I am here to stay,
and can't nobody take me away.

You brought me here from a distant land
and made me sweat and toil by hand.
Now, I'm back by popular demand
and can't nobody take me away!

You never thought that I'd be free.
Always thought you could get rid of me.
Bet you wished that I would flee,
but I am here to stay
and can't nobody take me away!

You see, I am the voice of 400 years
of heartaches, hopes, dreams, and fears.
Crying to a world where no one hears,
but I am here to stay
and can't nobody take me away!

BLACK ROSE

Black Rose, what's your name?
Black Rose, what's your claim to fame?
My beautiful Black Rose forever stay the same.
Black Rose,

You are the seeds of love, hope, and happiness.
Deeply mired in life's mud and filth and mess.
How you survived is anybody's guess.
Black Rose,

Watered by the tears of an entire race,
your roots grew and strengthened at a quickening pace.
Turn to the sun, so that I can see your face.
Black Rose,

Though dark storm clouds may brew and loom,
like a lotus when it is in full bloom
you rise in spite of impending doom
My strong Black Rose,

Have pride, smile wide, and glide in your black queenly ways.
Your beauty is so rare, you continue to amaze.
May you grace me with your beauty for the rest of my days.
Black Rose,

You have proven something not everyone knows.
That through adversity, great beauty grows.
You have given us a heritage so rich, it glows.
I will always cherish my beautiful Black Rose.

DESIRE

Another time, another place,
this story could have gone with some other face.
No place to stay...
just one more day.
I never thought that I'd be a runaway.

Put on some clothes, check out my face.
Find my mascara and I'm back in the race.
Just seventeen,
I'm trim an lean,
see my reflection and I'm still looking fierce.

Put on foundation
and I powder my nose.
Put on some fishnets
and practice my pose.
Check out my strut as I walk to the street.
Must keep an eye out as I'm walking my beat.

I paint my nails,
put on a tighter shirt.
Put on some lipstick
and hike up my skirt.
Put on some pumps as I walk out the door.
check out the scene, see what it's got in store.

I know the deal.
Who's my next meal?
I'm living low now, but I'd never steal.

I close my eyes and hear my family's voice.
Their cries are haunting me, but I had no choice.
I feel their tears.
I know their fears.
I won't go home until I'm in a Rolls Royce.

Pass by a church and I say a prayer.
Forgive me for all the sins that I did this year.
Once, pure like a dove.
Now, I've lost your love.
Please don't deny me entry when I'm above.

Bless all my family, keep them safe tonight.
Please let my parents know that I am alright.
Condemned to roam.
I can't go home.
Misunderstood and now I'll do what feels good.

I know it's wrong, but the feeling's so strong.
You wait a minute, then you've waited too long.
Turned from the light.
I've got a bite.
Took out his wallet and he's playing my song.

I only wanted them to say that it's true.
Was that a request that was too hard to do?
Now it's too late.
This is my fate.
I will do anything to hear "I Love You."

But your soul has grown cold
from the lies you've been told.
Who do you believe?
Desire.
Sweet as the tears of a dove.
Desire.
Selling your soul for love.

"You know what I want.
You know what I need.
You know you've got to give me anything that I please.
I need your tender touch...
need it so much.
Love me tonight
...just for tonight."

THE COLOURS OF ME

Who am I?
I am warmth in the winter,
new growth in the springtime,
and the cool breeze on a hot summer day.
I am all the colors of the fall.
Recognize me?

Well try again.
I am the epitome of elegance.
Trendy, sleek, and chic.
I always make my entrance grand.
I can be late and still be on time.
Did I get your attention?

That's all I wanted.
I've changed many times in my life.
I've gone from obscurity to world recognition,
Kente cloth to silk.
I've been a slave and a king,
but I never forgot who I was.

I've built the world's tallest buildings.
I've built the pyramids in Egypt.
I've even built an entire nation.
I've left riddles that will plague man for centuries.
I've been a doctor, a lawyer, a singer, a writer, a senator,
a congressman, winner of a Nobel Peace Prize...and a Pulitzer.
I am black, beautiful, and bolder than anyone you've ever met.
So I ask you...what was your question?

ANGELS AIN'T SUPPOSED TO CRY

Angels ain't supposed to cry
I never thought to question why
when people steal, kill, cheat, and lie,
are angels not supposed to cry.

Why in a land where beauty reigns
is the landscape painted with blood stains,
from chaffing skin against iron chains
...of people sold for financial gains.

Why in this world where man was made,
better yet, in a world where we all end up grayed
is there so much confusion over difference of shade?
The wounds may heal, but the scars won't fade.

God's precious canvas people taint,
with bones for brush and blood for paint.
His original creation is obscured and faint.
Thought angels' eyes were dry...but they ain't.

VANISHING (I CLOSE MY EYES)

I close my eyes
to all the crime that's rampant on the city streets.
Innocent's cries,
no more than ghostly waves lapping at my feet.
Social demise.
Can't take on the problems of everyone I meet.

Fading away,
everyone is fading away.
Gone like the wind,
everyone just fades with the wind.

I close my eyes,
and all of the injustice seems to fade away.
Naked skies,
clouds do not have a place in my mind today.
The falcon flies,
its eyes reflect the glory of a brand new day.

Fading away,
all the pain is fading away.
Gone like the wind,
all the pain just fades with the wind.

I close my eyes,
and life is now the way that it's supposed to be.
The falcon cries,
its voice heralds the dawning of my fantasy.
Consciousness rise,
there is no desolation and no tragedy.

Fading away,
all the pain is fading away.
Gone like the wind,
all the pain is gone with the wind.

I close my eyes
I'm blinded to the sorrow that's surrounding me.
Broken ties,
divorced from all the wrongs my brothers and sisters see.
My spirit dies,
I'm so alone and now there's no one there for me.

Fading away,
everyone is fading away.
Gone like the wind.
Everyone is gone with the wind.

ALL I'VE GOT

There was a time
when I had my hopes and dreams
and my world had come together as one.

Now in my life,
opportunity is gone
and my only roof is under the sun.

I feel as though
I see through a looking glass
and I pray the next life is a better one.

I still have faith
that a better day will dawn,
though all my dreams have faded into the sun.

They're all I've got.
They're all I've got in this world
and it's all the hope that I'll ever need.

They're all I'm not.
They're all I've wanted to be
and it's all the hope that I need.

Things come and go,
possessions are few and far between,
dignity was traded, no need for false pride.

Tattered and worn,
a change cup sits at my feet
and my clothes are ripped apart at the side.

People walk by.
They've acclimatized to me,
but they claim I take away city pride.

Unwanted on earth,
heaven must be a better place,
all my dreams fulfilled with God by my side.

It's all I've got.
It's all I've got in this world
and it's all the hope that I'll ever need.

It's all I'm not.
It's all I've wanted to be
and it's all the hope that I need.

AFTER THE RAIN

It took a while
for me to find
the strength to face the fact and recognize that our love
was really gone.
But you were wrong,
I am that strong,
I've found the strength inside, I'm over you and I am moving on.

After the rain,
I lived with the stain
that your treachery left on my love for you,
but I'm fine now.
I am.

There was a time
when I denied
the possibility of you loving anyone else but me,
but now my eyes
are opened wide.
I will not fight for something that wasn't meant to be.

After the rain,
I dealt with the pain,
licked my wounds and just tried to make it through,
but I'm fine now.
I am.

But, now and then,
can't block it out,
your tender touch, the memories of loving you flow through my mind.
You haunt my mind.
You steal my love.
When you come back you'll find your hold's broken,
the ties no longer bind.

After the rain,
it drove me insane,
but I've finally got back my life again,
and I'm fine now.
I am.

DON'T (WALK AWAY)

Don't tell me that you miss me.
That comes as no surprise.
Don't tell me that you're sorry.
I can see it in your eyes.

Don't tell me that you love me.
I've heard it all before.
Don't speak to me of honesty.
I don't trust you anymore.

Don't whisper to me gently.
Don't tell me any lies.
Don't tempt me with your sweet caress.
Don't ignore my silent cries.

Don't tell me that you know me.
Don't tell me that you care.
Don't use my weaknesses against me
while I'm lost within your stare.

Don't call me in the night.
Don't seduce me with your voice.
My love is not your right.
Just leave me with that choice.

Don't make me dream about you
and then just fade away.
Don't treat me like I'm second best...
that's not a role I play.

Don't speak of commitment
if you don't intend to stay.
Don't make me fall in love with you
and then just walk away.

LONELY

Don't you fear, oh no.
It's only me.
It's only me,
living my fantasy
when your love was only there to please me.
There waiting for me
like an open door, love rushed over me.
Embers of ecstasy
replacing you and me,
now that's a memory.

I've been lonely.
What am I supposed to do
with the memories
of loving you?
I've been lonely.
Close my eyes to visions of you.
The memory
of you and me
and me with you.

You can't waste
what you don't have.
Can't create want
even in me.
You were so fiery.
When the wind blows
I feel your touch.
Is it getting hot in here? In fact
it's only you.
It's only you.
Feel the heat,
the heat in your hand.
Don't you understand
I'll be loving you
in my memories.

I've been lonely.
What am I supposed to do
with the memories
of loving you?
I've been lonely.
Close my eyes to visions of you.
The memory
of you and me
and me with you.

Now it's all I have.
It's waiting for me.
When the rain falls
I feel your embrace
washing over me.
The silent kiss
of yesterday's bliss.
The memory
of you and me
Now I'm all alone.

QUIET STORM

I was walking in the rain.
Fog and mist surrounding me.
Closing in on every side,
this eerie silence won't let me be.

Tears of rain form on my face.
Stop the drizzling, just let it rain.
The clouds have opened up on me.
Cleanse my spirit, wash away my pain.

A chill had swiftly filled the air,
my coat was blowing in the wind.
Contemplating what I did.
Oh Father, how I've sinned.

Temptation overtaking me.
Her beauty blinding, I could not see.
Got my conscience telling me:
Don't trouble the water, just let it be.

We gave into sweet release.
Although our love should never be.
And the rain came tumbling down.
Don't stop the flow, wash over me.

Her bated breath, her trembling breast.
The rain makes me tremble beneath its touch.
As she lay across my chest.
Sweet caresses I miss so much.

Guilt and confusion play with my mind.
I'm living through all my worst fears.
I'll get the girl, lose my best friend.
Fate's been broken, release the tears.

Now, I don't know what to do.
This is not how it should be.
One night of love was all we shared.
Broken memories tormenting me.

The wind was blowing through my hair.
The wind had come, then suddenly died.
Darkness enveloping me.
Feeling alone and cold inside.

Thunder rolling on the hills.
Lightning added to the storm.
Insignificant and small,
the light of love does not keep me warm.

GOODBYE

Your love is leaving me so cold,
where once it made me safe and warm.
This love, it feels so very old,
it's lost its shape, but not its form.

My love for you grows very deep.
So deep it brought me to my knees.
The memories I'll always keep,
they flood my mind with cultured ease.

I thought this love would never end,
but it seems that I was wrong.
Although my spirit will not bend.
The memories will keep me strong.

I never knew that love brought pain,
but it's right here before my eyes.
The memories come down like rain.
Emptiness still clouds my skies.

I never thought that I would hear
another sad and twisted lie,
but now that's all that fills the air
and that is why I say goodbye.

EACH DAY THAT PASSES

Each day that passes
I try to cover the pain,
but in the cold winter silence
this emptiness comes down like rain.

Each day that passes
I know that life will go on,
but how can I make it
when all that I am living for is gone?

Each day that passes,
I don my normal disguise.
Through the bittersweet laughter
actions are betrayed by my eyes.

Each day that passes,
I cry, my tears are in vain.
The eyes of deliverance
look at me with such bitter disdain.

Each day that passes,
the hollowness inside of me grows.
The misery in me
haunts me more than anybody knows.

Each day that passes,
my soul is wrent in the flame.
The fire's still burning
eternally in your name.

Each day that passes,
people look but still they don't see
that my mind won't know silence
until you come back to me.

ALRIGHT...FOR YOU

Look in my eyes darling,

take a good look at me.

Why after all this time

is your love still haunting me?

But, that's alright...for you.

You were my fantasy.

I loved you endlessly.

Tell me that it's not true

after all that we've been through.

But, that's alright...for you.

I gave you everything.

Every part of me.

Now I have set you free,

but where does that leave me?

But, that's alright...for you.

FOR YOU MY SOUL CRIES

A slow fire burning.
You sit and I hold you tight.
Our bodies are yearning
to make this a special night.

We walk out to the beach
with a glass of wine.
The shore we do not reach
but everything turns out fine.

Sounds of nature waking,
the waves pound against the shore.
Your lonely heart aching,
haunted and wanting more.

I see your reflection
the sun rises in your eyes.
My heart needs protection,
but for you my soul cries.

NOBODY KNOWS

Voice in the dark.
A voice within me cries.
Spirit within.
The spirit within me dies.
Deep emotions
behind these reflecting eyes,
but nobody knows
the loneliness I disguise.

Thunder outside,
lightning flashes as it's storming.
Crackling fire,
keeps changing shape and then reforming.
Sentimental,
I think of you and my heart's warming,
but nobody knows
no one can stop these tears from forming.

Fire within.
This fire is still burning.
Lost memories.
Old feelings are returning.
Scarred by the past
my eyes are more discerning.
But nobody knows,
that for you, I'm still yearning.

CRYING ON CHRISTMAS EVE

My view is lonely,
missing you only.
Your reflection in an emptied glass of gin.

It seems the liquor
disappears quicker,
but since you've gone that's just the mood I'm in.

The birth of our Savior
still couldn't save your
sorry ass from spoiling my Holy Night.

Though this is bringing
a new beginning,
I know in time everything will be alright.

Your love was fleeting.
No New Year's greeting.
Calling out to a lonely half passed love.

So this is Christmas
well Merry Christmas
to you and your new love.

Society,
Sobriety,
wake me from a state where I forget the pain.

When I'm not drinking
I sit here thinking.
Memories of our love come down like rain.

Outside it's snowing.
The tears are flowing.
All the love I've given you and none to receive.

I'm by the fire.
I hear the choir.
Sitting alone crying on Christmas Eve.

WITHOUT YOU

Endless hours bind my restless heart

to this plane of existence.

My soul's disquiet cannot remain unheard for long

My ashes are scattered.

Will I ever be whole again?

Won't somebody help me?

Mind without body

Body without soul

Alive, but not living.

A shadow in a world of blinding light.

I find myself yearning

for the bittersweet ecstasy of eternal sleep

So I can lay my soul to rest

Sentenced to life without you, I wait

for the freedom of my final date

that has been predestined by God or Fate.

IN THE NIGHT

In the night,
hear the whispers of my call
as another teardrop falls.

In the night,
I can feel your sultry ways,
the essence of you stays.

In the night,
I see reflections of your face.
A sight no one can replace.

In the night,
I see danger in the skies
as I look into your eyes.

In the night,
I can feel your body's heat
as we share the same heartbeat.

In the night,
as the walls come closing in
and my soul is lost within.

In the night,
there is silence all around
as my tears fall to the ground.

In the night,
when I'm lying all alone
and my spirit starts to roam

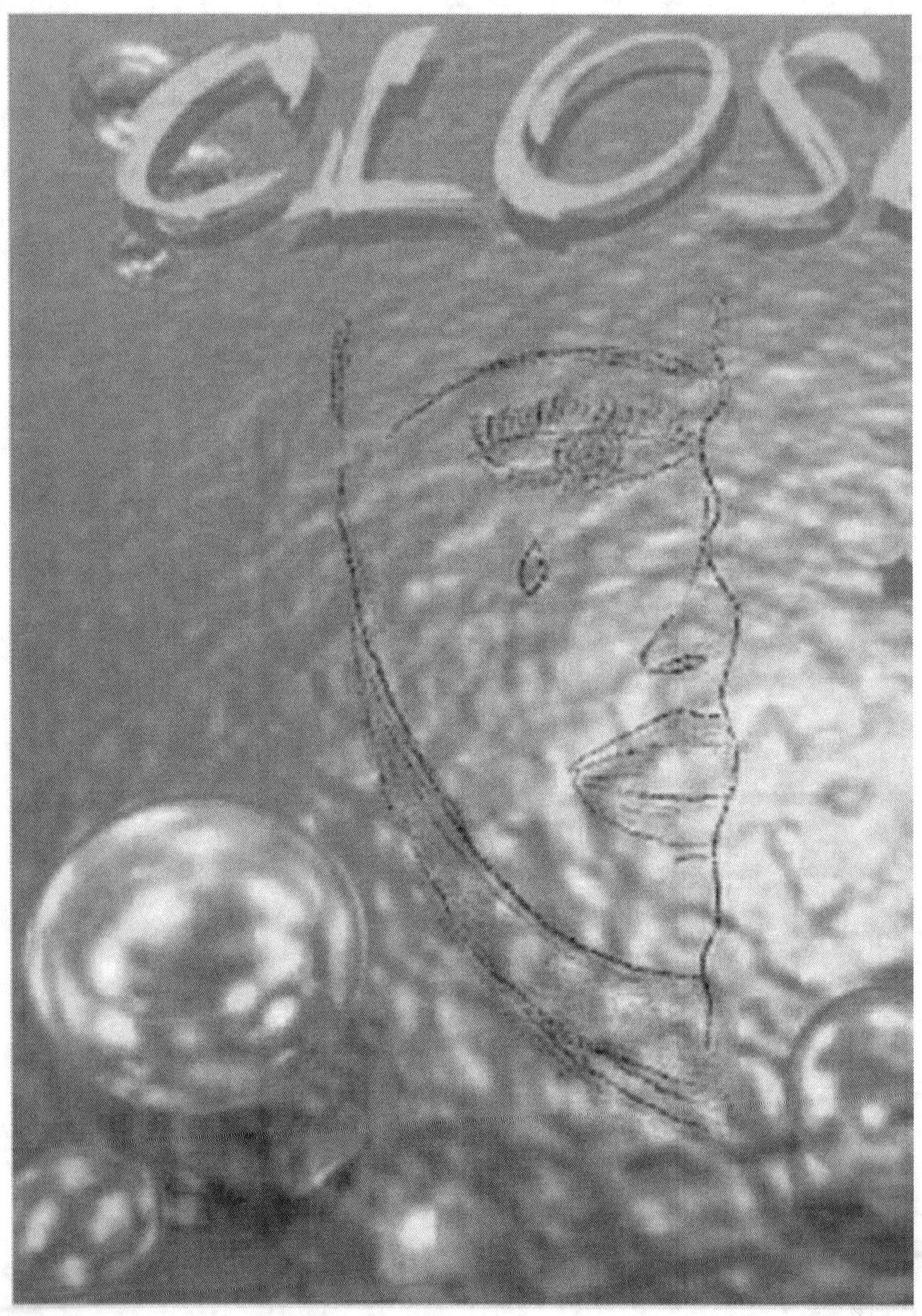

SHOULD I WAIT FOR YOU?

Stepped into the light,
when all is said and done.
It all became so crystal clear,
some wars cannot be won.
Water rushing blindly to shore
seeking its embrace.
Emotions flowing through the door,
I looked into your face
...and now I'm all alone

After all this time,
it's you I'm thinking of.
It's you I'm dreaming of.
It's still you that I love.
Should I wait for you?
it's you I'm thinking of.
It's you I'm dreaming of.
It's still you that I love.

Trapped inside the earth
praying for rebirth.
I'd follow you to distant lands.
My heart was in your hands.
Beneath hidden emotions,
Love's solar eclipse.
I feel the heat of your embrace,
the fire in your lips
but now I'm all alone.

After all this time,
it's you I'm thinking of.
It's you I'm dreaming of.
It's still you that I love.
Should I wait for you?
it's you I'm thinking of.
It's you I'm dreaming of.
It's still you that I love.

Faces of you
go rushing through my mind.
In solitude I hide
my love deep down inside.
As I wander through,
emotionally blind,
Love's leading me down this road
and still you're all I find.

Failed romances,
Circumstances,
Took my chances.
Changing faces,
Distant places,
Time erases.
Love's eclipse,
Relationships,
The fire in your lips.

After all this time,
it's you I'm thinking of.
It's you I'm dreaming of.
It's still you that I love.
Should I wait for you?
it's you I'm thinking of.
It's you I'm dreaming of.
It's still you that I love.

Time still finds you on my mind.
I just have to wonder.

UNDERSTAND ME

That's all I wanted.
Someone devoted,
someone stable
to give me life.

You left me haunted
and how I wanted
to be able
to give you life.

Treat me with the hands of a child.
Understand me.
Wake me from this state of denial.
Understand me.

Every hour,
love surrounds me.
I'm mistaken,
it's no disguise.

Lost in your power,
You have found me.
I am taken...
lost in your eyes.

Every day I try to deny
that I need you.
My love for you grows, I don't know why.
What do I do?

I'm so enraptured
by your devotion.
You don't notice
I'm mesmerized.

My soul, you've captured.
Rush of emotion.
You don't notice
I'm hypnotized.

Touch me like the light of the sun.
Understand me.
Can't you see you're the only one.
Understand me.

UNDERNEATH

Underneath the pale night sky
as autumn winds go rushing by
I see the look that's in your eye.
I start to cry
and say goodbye.

Underneath every smile
I wish you would stay a while.
Your eyes are like a sparkling wine
but you're not mine
and that's just fine.

Underneath my spirit dies.
There's pain behind these reflecting eyes.
My heart will heal, my tears will dry
but won't you try
to pacify.

Underneath the tears I cried,
I let go of the pain I hold inside.
Letting go of you, God knows I've tried
but I confide
you're still inside
underneath.

EVERY SINGLE MEMORY (VERSION 1)

Every single memory
has become a part of me.
And every single memory
is what you are to me.

And every single memory
has become my fantasy
And every single memory
says I love you endlessly.

And every single memory
is a mist surrounding me.
And every single memory
is a kiss from you to me.

And every single memory
leaves me longing endlessly.
And every single memory
drifts along a lovelit sea.

And every single memory
is of you embracing me.
And every single memory
is a light that shines on me.

And every single memory
is a dream that's haunting me.
And every single memory
is a spell you've cast on me.

EVERY SINGLE MEMORY (VERSION 2)

And every single memory
will lead you rushing back to me.
What will it take to make you see
that you and I were meant to be?

With every single memory
my mind is lost in ecstasy.
I think about you constantly,
but I know we will never be.

With every single memory
I see you fading distantly.
Your voice echoing so softly,
but you're not calling out to me.

And every single memory,
a picture painted so clearly.
I see my shattered fantasy.
Wash away the pain from me.

With every single memory,
a shadowed face replacing me,
but still my eyes can never see
that you are not in love with me.

CLOSER TO YOU

I often fantasize
my dreams will bring me closer to you.
That you will realize
my love is waiting right here for you.
Then you'll let me in your soul
and we will lose control.

If I could sell my soul
I would to bring me closer to you.
I'd surrender my life
for just one moment inside of you.
Unending fantasies, images of you.
They help to ease my mind, but won't see me through.

I feel your touch, your kiss,
my every thought is right here with you.
I would yield to the bliss
of knowing that you feel that way too.
I ache for just three words
but still they go unheard.

You'll never know the feelings
I am holding inside for you.
I long to lose control
and let my passion flow over you.
Visions of ecstasy, always on my mind.
I pray to be with you, but love's so unkind.

I can guess how you feel,
your scent, your taste, your everything.
I long to let you know
that this is not just another fling.
Just take the time to see
that you belong with me.

I know you think of me
very fondly, but just as a friend
I try to hide this love
inside of me, but I can't pretend.
Each time I speak to you I feel something new.
Someone can love you well but not like I do.

I know from your perspective
that this must come so suddenly.
I long to possess you,
my body aches just to set you free.
Just let me in your heart
then we can make a start.

I wish I was an angel
sent to guide and watch over you.
Whenever you're in need
I'd be the one that you would turn to.
Whatever you desire I will be to you.
I will do anything to get closer to you.

BROKEN VIEW

Keep running in and out my mind
constant fantasies of you.
I know that to my love you're blind,
but there's nothing I can do.

I have this growing pain inside,
but your touch will see me through.
My love is much to deep to hide
but you don't notice the view.

If you look deeply in my eyes
you'll see the longing in my soul.
Feelings I never could disguise,
but your kiss could make me whole.

Just take the time to look inside.
You will see the pain I feel.
To you my arms are open wide,
but I've got to know the deal.

If you don't love me let me know
and I'll gladly back away,
but if you love me let it show
decide if you want me to stay.

Don't leave me hanging for your love.
Don't leave me drowning in this pain.
'Cause we can fit like hand and glove.
You can shield me from the rain.

But I'm still drawing a blank line
and I need to know for sure.
How can I heal this pain of mine
when you are the cause and cure?

WHAT'S IT GONNA BE?

What's it gonna be
is love a dead end?
Tell me if you see
us more than just friends.

What's it gonna be?
Your eyes take my soul.
Take me discreetly,
envelop me whole.

What's it gonna be?
I ache for your touch.
Loving so carefree
I want you so much.

What's it gonna be?
Been waiting so long.
Feeling so lonely,
the nights are so long.

What's it gonna be?
I'm needing you so.
I can set you free,
but you'll never know.

What's it gonna be?
'Cause I can't hold on.
This love is all I see,
don't wait 'til I'm gone.

HOLD ME

Hold me tight and don't let go.
You've got a touch that rocks my soul.
You must surrender to the flow,
inhibition will take its toll.
So take your time and do it slow.
We've got all night to reach our goal.

We've got to make sure this love lasts.
We must allow this love to grow.
Don't make me rush. Don't go too fast.
Ecstasy in time you'll know...
Sweet memories lost in the past.
Just hold me tight and don't let go.

Hold me tight and don't let go.
I feel the heat of your embrace.
Your tender touch I long to know.
I close my eyes and see your face.
If you love me let it show.
We've got a love time can't erase.
Just hold me tight and don't let go.

I'M SHAKING

Ground-breaking
soul-shaking
love-making
I'm reeling
concealing
this feeling.

Time-chasing
embracing
heart-racing
mind-aching
soul-quaking
I'm shaking.

Defenses
pretenses
lost senses
possession
confession
discretion.

Ecstasy
fantasy
follow me
back-breaking
mind-raking
I'm shaking.

HOW CAN I LET YOU KNOW?

Standing in this silence
my words just melt forever.
How can I say what I feel?
I long to bridge the distance
and share your love forever.
How can I show you it's real?

And though,
there are so many things that
I would die to tell you.
How can I let you know?

If you could see the feelings
I have for you this moment
I don't know what I would do.
How many years I've waited
each waking moment I've spent
trying to get through to you.

And though,
there is nobody else
I'd give my love to
How can I let you know?

Hanging on your words,
my love dangling in the balance
and still I'm waiting for you.
Watching every movement
to see if I stand a chance
but still no response from you.

And though,
my words will only limit
my feelings for you.
How can I let you know?

IN YOUR EYES

I feel your sadness
reaching blindly through this madness.
It's in your eyes.
Distantly shining,
like the horizon underlining
when sunlight dies.

A revelation
melted this icy confrontation
when your eyes shine.
More than possession,
your eyes betray a true confession.
Just like mine.

You heard me calling.
Too late to save me I have fallen
into your eyes.
Telling your story
just like an angel's shining glory.
It's in your eyes.

Silent devotion,
like rivers running to the ocean.
It's in your eyes.
It's just a token,
although my love still goes unspoken.
It's in my eyes.

ONE DAY

Maybe one day
we'll end this journey.
Someway,
time will bring you to me
and you'll stay
forever in my arms.

I watch the sun rise
shining so brightly
like your eyes
I stare into nightly.
No disguise
could ever hide your charms.

Spread your wings and just fly away.
Our hearts were meant to meet another day
and if by chance we're not destined to be
my love for you will be my memory
spread your wings and fly
don't say goodbye.

At night the sun sets
white fire burning.
Colors melt
slowly in yearning.
Won't you let,
let me in your soul.

Piercing the sky
the moon rises boldly
in your eyes.
I just wish you would hold me.
The time flies,
just let love take control.

Spread your wings and just fly away.
Our hearts were meant to meet another day
and if by chance we're not destined to be
my love for you will be my memory
spread your wings and fly
don't say goodbye.

And maybe one day
we'll end this silence
and you'll say
that you'll give me a chance.
I replay
that moment in my mind.
Is it a fantasy
that you'll return to me.
Destiny
is guiding our journey
and maybe
we are two of a kind.

NEVER CHANGE

Sun is up
and the moon is sinking.
Night withdraws
as the day begins.
By the stream
the deer is drinking.
Feel the wind
touch against my skin.

Clouds move in
and the sky is crying.
Frightened waves
running to the shore.
Take my heart
there is no denying
that our love's
not what it was before.

Things have seemed to change so fast.
All that was familiar is in the past.
I tell you I will always hold you near.
They say that things change, my dear.

Mountains crumble
as the earth is shifting.
Mighty kingdoms
vanish in the sands.
Flower petals
on the sea are drifting.
Carry seeds
to far off distant lands.

Winter cries
as the spring is dying.
Trees once lush
now have nothing to show.
Raging storm
and the birds are flying.
Seeking shelter
in the trees below.

Things have seemed to change so fast.
All that was familiar is in the past.
I tell you I will always hold you near.
They say that things change, my dear.

Mirror, Mirror
what a sad reflection.
Species vanish
with the rising sun.
Oceans dry,
rivers change direction.
Canyons forming
where the river runs.

Winter melts,
oceans form between us.
Now two islands
where there once was one.
As we drift
emptiness has seen us.
Darkness slowly
blocking out the sun.

Things have seemed to change so fast.
All that was familiar is in the past.
I tell you I will always hold you near.
They say that things change, my dear.

Deserts grow
where oceans once stood proud.
People age,
cultures rise and fall.
Vapor rises
to form the sleeping cloud.
Dormant seeds
now stand proud and tall.

Tears will fall,
just as many will dry
as I bid farewell
to my first love.
Beauty fades,
but true love cannot die.
I wish you all the love
you're dreaming of.

Things have seemed to change so fast.
All that was familiar is in the past.
I tell you I will always hold you near.
They say that things change, my dear.
Never Change.

WHAT DO I DO?

I see the look in your eye
and know that it is telling no lie.
I fade as you pass my side
reaching out for you, but still I'm denied.

I pray for you every day
and love you in my own special way.
It should come as no surprise.
I'm sure you can see through my thin disguise.

If you would only be mine,
the world we shared would be truly divine.
Although I know from the start
that I need to find a way into your heart.

Your love is endless and strong
and it shouldn't take long
until you're here by my side.
There's nowhere to hide.
My love burns in your name
I'm dying, lost in its flame.
What do I do?

I wake up wishing you near,
but moonlight is the only thing there.
I dream of holding you tight
hoping that this dream will replay tonight.

At night I stare at the sea
praying that it can bring you to me.
Like waves seek refuge at shore
my love is here and that's what it's for.

If you would only be mine,
the world we shared would be truly divine.
Although I know from the start
that I need to find a way into your heart.

Your love is endless and strong
and it shouldn't take long
until you're here by my side.
There's nowhere to hide.
My love burns in your name
I'm dying, lost in its flame.
What do I do?

AS I NEED YOU

Mist clears
then I saw you standing there.
What is it you seek?
The air will not speak
the answers that you need.

I'm here
in the shadows lost in fear.
Blindly reaching out
through the screams of my self-doubt.
Hoping to be seen.

Broken hearts
often have some missing parts.
What will complete me?
What will end this misery
and fill this aching need?

In your eyes,
the echoes of your silent cries.
Calling out to me
begging me to set you free
as I need you.

IS THIS HOW IT ENDS?

As time goes by, I'm waiting
desperately hoping for change.
Was I born to lose
my heart, my love, my life, my destiny.
Was this the way it had to be?

Do you believe?
Believe love is strong,
one of a kind,
a better place to share our lives?
Or is there nothing to find?

How could someone,
someone like me,
so strong and hopelessly independent
fall in love so completely?
And who would have thought that
your love would set me free.
Is this how it ends?

Do you believe?
Believe in destiny
and in love again?
It's not the way it has to be.
Is this how it ends?

ALWAYS

Always a haunting vision.
Always a memory
to bring you back to me.
Feel like I'm in a prison.
Won't you please set me,
set me free.

Time brought our hearts together.
Now time has taken you,
has taken you away.
You're in my heart forever
memories revisit
every day.

Is this the end?
Why can't I let go
of the feelings I am clinging to?
I just can't pretend.
Every road I travel
leads right back to you.

Always a tear that's falling
washing endlessly,
washing over me.
Always your voice that's calling.
Echoing silently
overtaking me.

Always a bridge that's burning.
Keeping you here with me,
Keeping you here with me.
Always this endless yearning
softly, distantly,
bringing you back to me.

Is this the end?
Why can't I let go
of the feelings I am clinging to?
I just can't pretend.
Every road I travel
leads right back to you.

TELL ME WHAT YOU NEED

Just tell me what you need
and I will be there.
My aching heart would bleed
just to ease your fear.

I'll be whatever you desire.
Inspire you a little higher.

Just tell me what you need.
I ache to possess you.
I long to set you free
hold and caress you.

I'll be whatever you desire.
You've got all night to light my fire.

Just tell me what you need.
I'm trapped by desire.
This heat is all I need.
I'm lost in this fire.

I'll be whatever you desire.
Who knows what magic you'll inspire.
...just tell me what you need.

ONE MORE TEAR

Colors fade
and the night has fallen.
Feel your touch
and my spirit's freed.
One more year,
One more tear has fallen.
Cleanse my soul
but, don't drown the seed.

Night sets in,
I embrace it gladly.
Night protects me
as it holds me near.
Shining stars
shine upon me sadly.
Midnight clouds
shield me from their stare.

Time should heal
but the wound grows deeper.
Light of day
puts me to the test.
Reaching out
but the shadows keep her.
Lay her down,
put her soul to rest.

Seasons fade
and the spring is dawning.
Flowers bloom
where our feet once tread.
Morning dew
and the rose is yawning.
Spreads her petals
and she rests her head.

Time goes on,
shadows fall upon me.
Abandoning me
to the light of day.
Think of how
you stole my heart from me.
Now it beats
for you every day.

Thunder rolls
and the wind gets stronger,
rain is slowly
falling in the night.
See your smile
as the days get longer.
Feel your heat
as you hold me tight.

Sun descends
as the day gets older.
See the sadness
as the daylight dims.
Emptiness
as the days get colder.
Feel your breath
burning on my skin.

Hair is gray
and my heart's still yearning.
Taste your kiss
as the snow sets in.
Time goes by
and the world's still turning.
Holding on
just to start again.

I HEAR YOUR VOICE

I snuggle up in the memories of you.
Tucked away, I feel safe and secure.
What had left me has returned.
I look at you and your smile makes me laugh.
The sound of your voice
brings back feelings I'd never hoped to feel again.
I feel like a child.
I hear your voice calling out to me.
I turn to speak and there's no one there.

THE BRIDGE

Scattered memories litter the floor of my mind.
My mind is alive with thoughts of you,
unlocking parts of me that seemed lost forever.
Swept away in some forgotten corner
until time healed the wounds that it inflicted.

Sorrow is a demon within me,
forcing out emotions that I long to repress
From the dying embers of my flame
I see a past blurred by tears
as my star rose only to eclipse yours much too soon.

Recalling Sundays in the park.
You were always on the mark.
Tell me why I'm sitting here all alone in the dark.
Time brought you to me,
now time has taken you away.

The earth has claimed your body.
God has claimed your soul.
I've nothing but memories of loving you.
Separated by more than distance...
the past is our only link.

SHATTERED EYES (TELL ME WHAT YOU SEE)

Looking out upon a world
as cold and dark as my lonely heart.
I see a world that's disenchanted,
disconnected, and apart.

What evil lurks inside a man
Who's sacrificed humanity?
If only they could bare their souls
to see what I can see...

A world full of sorrow.
A world full of regret.
A world where pain and misery
come together and beget.

And while filled with this mystery,
I see why God has chosen me
and I reject this apathy, tell me what you see.

You can see inside me.
Do you see what I see?
I'm looking at the world through shattered eyes.

What evil lurks beside you?
What demon's in your mind?
Open up the door to truth
and that is what you'll find.

There is no place to run to.
There is no place to hide.
To find the pain you're running from
you need just look inside...

A world full of injustice,
where words are weapons to deploy.
A world that's rushing to me
to deliver or destroy.

And while blinded by reality,
I look upon humanity.
Through the pieces of my shattered eyes, tell me what you see.

EYES OF A LOST SOUL

Look upon me and know who I am.
When you call out for help
it is my name you speak.
When you reach in the darkness
it is my hand you seek.
Look into my eyes and find the knowledge that you seek.
The eyes of a lost soul don't lie.
Look upon me and know who I am.
I am hope.
I am tranquility.
I am serenity.

Look upon me and know who I am.
When you're lying all alone
it is my face that you see.
When you locked away your heart
it was I who held the key.
It is my smile that warms you.
It is my breath that keeps you cool.
Look into my eyes and find the strength when you are weak.
The eyes of a lost soul don't lie.
Look upon me and know who I am.
I am past.
I am present.
I am the future.

Look upon me and know who I am.
When you're embraced by another
it is my touch that you feel.
When your dream was just a vision
it was I who made it real.
Look into my eyes and see your destiny.
The eyes of a lost soul don't lie.
Look upon me and know who I am.
I am strength.
I am unity.
I am yours.

REDEMPTION

A familiar face
a long forgotten touch.
The cold sting of winter
never seared so much.

My mind's gone astray.
My soul lost within
as I look for redemption
for all my past sins.

Haunted by sorrow
as I walk down the street.
Ghosts of my past
on every face I meet.

As I walk by the river
searching for truth.
The pain of remembrance.
The scars of my youth.

EYES OF DELIVERANCE

Eyes of deliverance
shine your light on me.
Give me the power
to set myself free.

Free of self-hatred.
Free of self-doubt.
Freed by the vision
to see my way out.

Look at this face
and calm all its fears.
Strip it of the burdens
its aching soul bears.

Torment and guilt
just won't let me be.
With your saving grace
please deliver me.

SET ME FREE

It's not my business to decide
what's your reality.
The sights you see aren't mine.
Only what the world can see.

I ask that you try to look beyond that
and have the courage to look upon me.

Not bound by convention.
Not bound by bitter lies.
Not bound by class or color.
Only by your eyes.

I accept this vulnerability,
knowing you can see through me
because I believe that you possess
the power to set me free.

ONE MOMENT

I was love and I was fear
I was flying through the air
on a ride as wild as night
as cold as rain
I shone so bright.
I dimmed the stars
with my burning light
at that one moment.

I was pure and I was free
of every insecurity.
I felt so proud that I was me
at that one moment.

I was bold and I was sage
My speech was years beyond my age
I released my pent up rage
and rewrote every tattered page
of history from a new perspective
at that one moment.

I never knew what I could do
Always thought it was up to you.
Days of confusion and doubt were through
at that one moment.

FRUIT OF FORGETFULNESS

Fruit of forgetfulness.
What fruit it bears.
God only knows the truths it hears.
Untold secrets
and whispered fears
falling upon deaf ears.

Fruit of forgetfulness.
What bittersweet tears.
God only knows of the sorrow you bear.
Innocence lost
and sins you can't share.
Healing the wounds of wasted years.

WINDS OF CHANGE

Winds of change
take to flight
lightning quick,
make your move,
strike tonight.

Power of thunder
show your might.
Rescue me,
hear my plea
feel my plight.

Eternal flame,
burning bright.
Come to me,
Set me free,
give me sight.

Tides have turned,
bare your bite
Raging currents
pound the shore,
the time is right.

LOST

Lost in thought, I am struck from all sides.

Conflicting visions of grandeur and demise shadow my every step.

My words echo the sighs of an aching soul.

Give me wings.

TAKE MY HAND

Take my hand
another day is dying.
Understand
That time's not ours for buying.

Without you my world is filled with silence,
the sound of broken memories is more than I can stand.

I'm on my own.
I walk this world in longing.
All alone,
no sense of real belonging.

Without you my soul is filled with sorrow.
Control of my emotion is no more at my command.

Take my hand,
your touch is everlasting,
in this land
where sense is often fleeting.

Without you my heart is cold and silent.
With every beat I hope we'll meet, but you're not there.

I'm on my own.
I fade into my sorrow.
On my own,
just praying for tomorrow.

Without you, the sound of aching silence.
The tender wings that carried me have gone and flown away.

Take my hand.
Caress my soul with your love.
Take my hand
and know it's you I think of
...when I'm on my own.

FALLEN ANGEL

Struck down by thunder.

A world torn asunder.

From valley low to mountain high

nothing is heard except the death cry

of the fallen angel.

FRIEND

The cold air of silence,
What was familiar is gone.
Conversation seems foreign,
Routine keeps moving on.

Though the words are unspoken,
The feelings are there.
But, the bond has been broken
and I can't help but fear.

Has something gone wrong?
Is the friendship in danger?
My doubts are so strong.
You feel like a stranger.

People talk about me
both night and day.
It seems my name comes up
whenever I'm away.

How they get started
is more than I can say,
but I couldn't help but notice
that you always seem to stay.

Silence is golden,
except in my defense.
Why you always listen
is starting to make sense.

I find out accidentally
of what is being said:
clips behind my message board,
overheard while I'm in bed.

Too petty for my nature,
I brought it to an end,
but what hurt me the most
was that it came from a friend.

ANGEL IN THE STORM

There's an angel in the storm
as it tries to change its form.
As it flies,
escape is its only goal
in the silent winter's cold.

Rain on my windowpane.
Clouds in the skies.
I see danger reflected
as I stare into your eyes.

As the mist begins to rise
the tormented angel cries.
As it flies,
trying to escape this pain,
but the emptiness remains.

Painful reminders.
Mind, body, and soul.
Once surrendered yourself
now your soul has grown cold.

As the tears fall in the rain
trying to silence its pain.
As it flies,
heading to the raging storm
only faith to keep it warm.

Circumstance and speculation,
turned away from the light,
now seeking redemption
as it flies into the night.

DO YOU BELIEVE?

Do you believe in my power?
Do you believe I tell you lies?
To find the truth you're searching for
look deeply in my eyes.

And right while you are looking there,
lost within my tender stare,
think of what I ask of you
and answer if you dare.

Your eyes do not threaten.
Your eyes have not revealed,
the contents of their mystery,
the power that they wield.

And while I'm flooded with this fear,
I shed another silent tear,
Because I believe that I possess
the answer to your prayer.

I know not of what you're thinking.
Know not of what you hear.
I only know that I possess
a power that you fear.

Though bound by insecurity,
you are the one that's right for me.
Do you believe that I possess
the power to set you free?

WON'T SOMEBODY HELP ME?

Imprisoned by my own device,

insecurities keep me bound

in a world as cold as ice,

Alone with the pain I've found.

In whom do I confide

that I'm dying on the inside?

Won't somebody help me?

DARKNESS OF LOVE (VERSION 1)

Love is a shadowy mist,
a vast unknown
where we all exist.
The landscape's barren and dark.
What can be seen,
sharp, contrasting, and stark.
I feel a sense of unease,
ill at heart
in the cold winter's breeze.
I look around in the dark.
The silence shrill,
but for the song of a lark.
I see the light in your eyes,
although there is no light from the skies
And so I cling to the light,
my salvation
from the terrors of night.
I'm ignorant of the source,
unwittingly
letting love take its course.
Suddenly caught in your stare
unable to move,
I tremble with fear.
I look at love with great fear,
its thundering voice
remains all that I hear.
I see more eyes up above,
Another one caught
in the darkness of love.

BARRIERS

Barriers
Rising all around.
Barriers
Keep me from being found.
Barriers
Blocking off my view.
Barriers
Prevent me from loving you.
Barriers
Just listen and you'll hear.
Barriers
Whispers of my fear,
Barriers
of losing all that I hold dear.
Barriers
Reminders of the past.
Barriers
How long will the scars last?
Barriers
Imprinted on my mind.
Barriers
Everywhere you look you'll find.
Barriers
That will haunt me 'till the dawn.
Barriers
Keeping me from moving on.
Barriers
Can't continue 'till they're gone.

GUARDIAN ANGEL

Guardian angel,
your presence by my side
is like a lullaby
and I
hear whispers of loves gone by.
Answer my silent cry.
Lift my heart to the sky.

As I close my eyes
I sit and I pray for the day
that you'll take me away.
As my body lies,
images of magic and wonder
dance behind my eyes.

Guardian angel,
I wake up in your warm embrace
as the sun hits your face
and I
look to the golden star
like looking at you from afar
I love you as you are.

As I close my eyes
I sit and I pray for the day
that you'll take me away.
As my body lies,
images of magic and wonder
dance behind my eyes.

THE GIFT

I remember how it felt
to have you sleeping in my arms.
So fragile and so innocent
in all your tender charms.

The part of life I've given you
is now mine to behold.
The journey of your lifetime
is a story yet untold.

Now that you are getting older.
All the lessons you will learn.
As the setting sun grows colder,
the tide has slowly turned.
The one that I gave life gives life to me.

As I watch you from the shadows
like the moon follows the sun.
I am always watching over you
wherever you may run.

As I watch you from the shadows
I will try to set you free.
The gift of life I gave to you
is now your gift to me.

Though my instinct is to protect you,
I will not deny you life.
The world's yours to experience
with all it's stress and strife.

I'm the angel's breath beneath your wings
whether you rise or fall.
I will be your inspiration
standing by you through it all.

IT'S MY TURN

I can guess at the emotions
that you felt when I was born,
the center of your universe
to love and to adorn.

The child you cradled endlessly
has grown before your eyes.
The love you gave has molded
me more than you realize.

Now that I am getting older.
All the lessons I have learned.
The pain of letting go grows colder,
But this wisdom I have earned:
To love another you must set them free.

It's my turn to tell you
not to let your spirit bend.
You were more than just a parent,
you have always been my friend.

Its' my turn to tell you
just how special you are to me.
The light that shines within me
is the love you gave to me.

Release the fear and sorrow
as your baby leaves the nest.
The wisdom you have given me
will help me pass the test.

Though it seems something is ending,
it has only just begun.
Sifting through the cherished memories
you are the only one.

REMEMBER

And if I should ever go away,
find a time that made you smile
and you remember me that way.
Promise me that you'll remember.

And though our time comes to an end
and it tears me up inside,
but I will always be your friend,
even if you don't remember.

I'm there, even though you cannot see
and you know that you will be
just as much a part of me
Memories I will remember.

I know, there are things I must confess
I will love you in a way
that words could never express
I hope you will remember.

And though, it's impossible to stay,
look into your heart and know
I'll think of you every day.
Your love I will remember.

And if we must be apart today
It is to you that I owe
a debt that I cannot repay
I will always remember.

And if a tear escapes my eye
These are tears of joy I cry
This could never be goodbye
You, I'll always remember.

NO REGRETS

There's a time to grow
and a time for living.
We can't go back and undo what's been done.
We can only hope
time is forgiving
'cause where we are must come second to none.

Time and time
I sit and I pray
for the strength
to carry-on today.

Burdened by the past.
Fearful of the future.
I lived my life in shadows of my pain.
Wounded by mistakes,
faith is my suture
experience will shield me from the rain.

Bound by fear
'till nothing else remained,
insecurity
was driving me insane.

Some will stand by you,
some will undermine you.
You can't be sure, it's a dangerous game.
Some will put you down,
some will wine and dine you.
Friends must be true before they earn that name.

Time has healed
what life ripped and tore
and the pain inside
won't hurt me anymore.

No apologies.
Begets pain and sorrow.
From the ashes I will surely rise above.
So I turn to those
with the strength to borrow.
Finally free to experience love.

Like a bird
I drift on the breeze.
No regrets, no sorrows,
my mind is at ease.

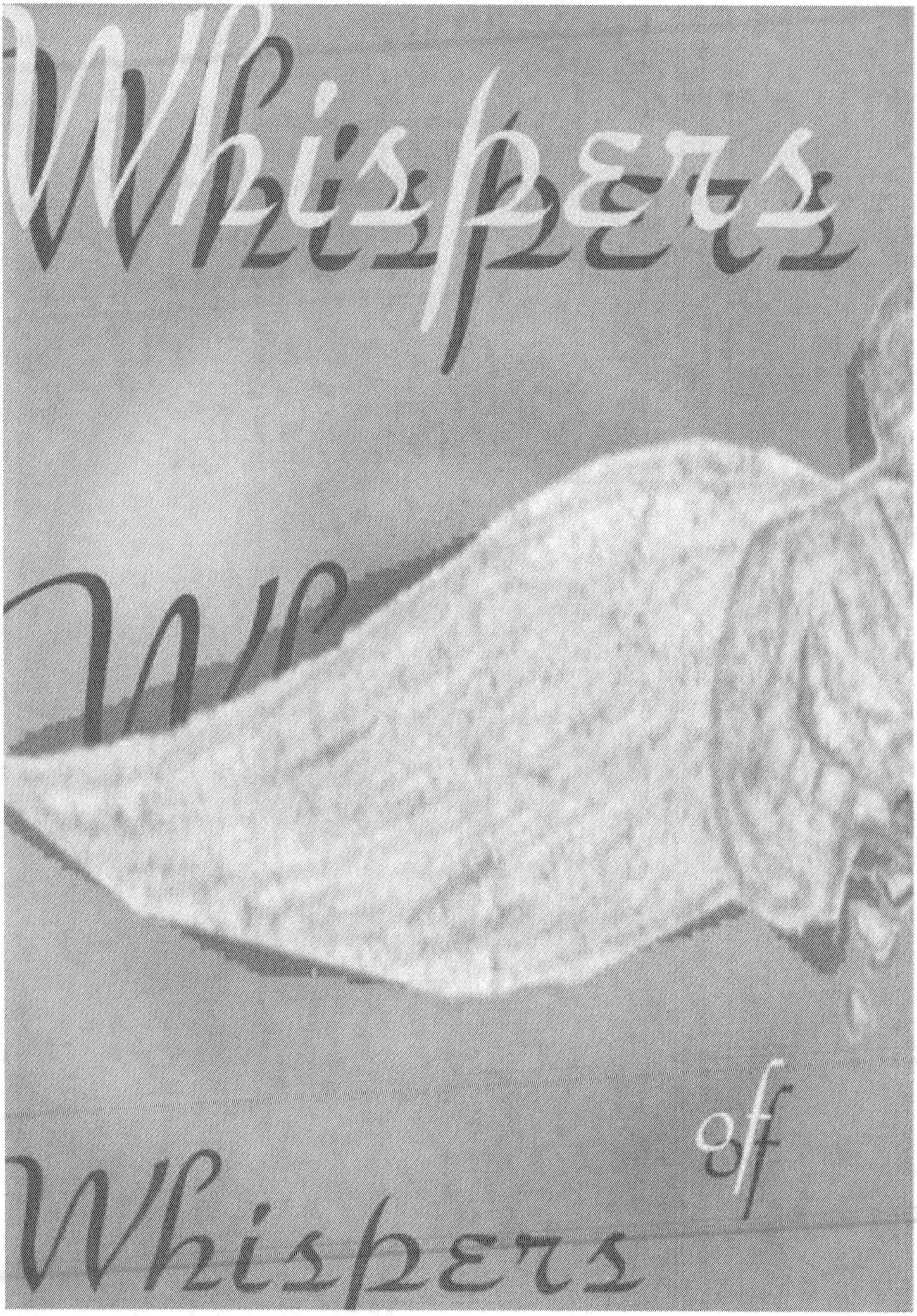

PRECIOUS ONE

Standing in silence,
emotions so deep.
I treasure this moment endlessly.

As you touch me so sweetly,
that look in your eyes
A look of belonging
you can't disguise.

Precious one
love me so deeply
love me completely
tonight

Confess
your love to me
always searching
now you've found me.
You have my heart,
my everything,
feeling you now
is all I really need.

Breaking the silence,
I don't say a word.
I know from your response
that you have heard.

Trembling as you come near me.
You whisper my name.
I know from this moment
things aren't the same.

Precious one
pray to me softly
you haven't lost me
tonight.

Confess
your love to me
always searching
now you've found me.
You have my heart
my everything
Feeling you now
is all I, all I really need.

LONGING

Longing,
wanting,
waiting,
haunted by visions of love.

Your voice
calling
to me
echoes softly through the night.

Tossing,
turning,
yearning,
burning for your tender kiss.

Drifting,
slowly
sinking
lost within your warm embrace.

Rising,
just like
fire
take me higher with your love.

Dreaming,
waking,
longing,
aching just to feel your touch.

COULD I EVER DESERVE YOU?

Could I ever deserve you?
If I could be your teardrops,
I'd wash away all of your pain
and bathe you in my love.
If I could be a puzzle
I would be the one missing piece
that makes you whole again.
If I could be a star,
I would set the heavens ablaze
so you'd notice me.
If I could be a flower,
I'd bloom in the warmth of your light
and fade each time you looked away.
If I could be time,
I'd rewind every moment with you
and live through them forever.
And if you were ever lost,
I'd lead you with my guiding light
until you're safe again.
If I had one wish,
I would be the light of day
so I could touch you once more.
If I could trade my heart
for something that didn't love you so much
so that I could live without you, I would.
Could I ever deserve you?

SOME SAY LOVE

Some say love, it is a current
that takes us out to sea.
Some say love, it is an angel
that visits you and me.
I say love, it is a shadow
that hovers over me.
Some say love, it is a storm cloud
that drowns us in its rain.
Some say love, it is a fabric
that bears a hidden stain.
I say love, it is a teardrop
that washed away my pain.
Some say love, it is a blanket
that keeps us warm at night.
Some say love, it is a garden
that grows back after blight.
I say love, it is vast darkness
with you it's guiding light.
Some say love, it is the first ray
of sunlight at the dawn.
Some say love, it is a pathway
that keeps us moving on.
I say love, it is a feeling
that sustains me when you're gone.

WHISPERS OF YOU

Unyieldingly,
fantasies of you
just flow into my mind.
Unendingly,
try to break free,
but you're the only escape I find.

What am I to do?
I'm so lost in you, baby.
Everything I do
whispers of you.
Every memory
brings you back to me.
You're my destiny.
Whispers of you.

Quarter 'til three.
You're all I see
as I stare at the sky 'til morning light.
Took time to see
you're all I need
and I secretly want to lose this fight.

Tell me where you are
so I can bring you to me.
Whether near or far
you're right here with me.

What am I to do?
I'm so lost in you, baby.
Everything I do
whispers of you.
Every memory
brings you back to me.
You're my destiny.
Whispers of you.

WISHES

Wish I was an angel,
I'd lift you on my wing.
Wish I was a bird,
only for you I'd sing.

Wish I was a dream,
I'd meet you every night.
Wish I was the sun,
so each day I'm your first sight.

Wish I was a star,
I'd guide you with my light.
Wish I was a gem,
I'd shine for you so bright.

But, I'm none of those
and wishes do just fade away,
like love.
So I'll never feel this way,
maybe I'm wrong, it's been so long.
Someday.

Wish I was a child,
I'd play with you each day.
Wish I was your heart,
I'd know just what to say.

Wish I was a tree,
I'd save you from the rain.
Wish I was a shield,
protect you from all pain.

Wish I was a toy,
I'd bring you so much joy.
Wish I was a man,
and not a frightened boy.

But, I'm none of those
and wishes do just fade away,
like love.
So I'll never know of love,
and what it is, and what it's not.
Dreams away.

WHAT IF (MY LOVE)

What if my love was much more than just words?
What if my love was all you saw, felt, and heard?
What would you do with it?

What if my
love was the rain when it's stormy?
Would you run away
or would you reach gently for me?
What if my
love was the sun in the morning?
Would you greet me with a kiss
or fade away without warning?

What if my
love was a dove in the moonlight?
Would you capture me
or would you help me to take flight?
What if my
love was a star in the night skies?
Would I fade in the dark
or would I shine in your eyes?

What if my
love was the warmth of a fire?
Would you put me out
or raise my temperature higher?
What if my
love was the sound of the ocean?
Would the water be calm
or constantly in motion?

What if my
love was the caress of a cool breeze?
Would it chill your soul
or set you at ease?
What if my
love was the tear of an angel?
Would it be shed in vain
or bathe you as it fell.

INSIDE MY MIND

I've prepared for this moment in my mind.
Whatever words were needed, I'd always find.
You'd sit across from me and stare in my eyes.
No matter what we talk about, the time just flies.

I long to feel your tender loving stare
and see the sunlight glisten through your hair.
I've imagined exactly how you feel.
I've felt your kiss so often, I'd swear it's real.

There'd be a time when speech transcends all words,
where words may not be spoken, but still are heard.
You look at me and your eyes start to glow.
My body calls out to you, "Take it slow."

I conjure up the scent of your perfume,
a smell so sweet I can't forget fills the room.
My muscles tense as you start coming near.
The gentle kiss you blow to me is all I hear.

You come and slowly take me by the hand.
You don't know, but your every wish is my command
Your kiss, it melts and freezes just the same.
I tremble every time I hear you call my name.

I can't resist your sweet and sultry ways.
You're the kind of girl for which every man hopes and prays.
You pull me close and then we start to dance.
Our feet move to the rhythm of our romance.

But, the courage to approach you I can't find.
I will always love you inside my mind.

FOR ALL THE THINGS I'VE NEVER SAID

Your kiss is like a summer breeze.
Your caress puts my soul at ease.
Like flowers in the morning dew,
I've grown because of loving you.

They say let young hearts run free.
You were there to complete me.
If I lived my whole life through
ain't nobody like you.

My love will echo
from every mountain high
and valley low.
Now you just let it flow.

For all the things I've never said.
For all the things inside my head.
For all the days I've let slip by.
For all the simple reasons why
I'll love you in a special way
I'll love you 'til my dying day.

Your love is like a melody.
Your gentle touch has set me free.
I guarantee to bring you joy
'cause I will always be your boy.

Once you were my fantasy.
Now you are reality.
Like an angel from above
you gave me your love.

Words cannot express
just what it is that I
want you to know.
I've got to let it show.

For all the things I've never said.
For all the things inside my head.
For all the days I've let slip by.
For all the simple reasons why
I'll love you in a special way
I'll love you 'til my dying day.

I MAY NOT KNOW

Baby, baby, baby,
must have cast a spell on me.
Please release me baby,
don't have the strength to set you free.

Every time I try,
time seems to bring you back to me
and I don't know why,
maybe this was meant to be.

I may not know
where I'm going to
or why I need you
to follow me
but I do.

Guiding like an angel
your love has completed me.
Every time you need me,
by your side is where I'll be.

Your eyes are white like fire
and they burn into my soul.
Searching through the darkness
you are the light that makes me whole.

I may not know
where I'm going to
or why I need you
to follow me
but I do.

Slowly wake in yearning
colors melt into the sun.
Memories keep my mind turning,
but you are the only one.

Falling into heaven,
you were there to break my fall.
I am yours forever
I'll be giving you my all.

THE WALL

I will be your wall.
When the water's too rough,
when the world is unkind,
when the fire and loss
leave you frightened and blind,
I will be your wall.

The rock you can lean on
for protection and defense.
To lift you to your higher ground
when my service to you ends.
I will be your wall.

My borders won't confine you...
Love's boundaries aren't set.
Seek refuge in my solitude.
Find peace without regret.
I will be your wall.

May sadness never find you.
May past failures grant you rest.
Find your fortress in my solitude
when life puts you to the test.
I will be your wall.

Let my touch unlock your passion.
Let my kiss give you new life.
Let my smile be inspiration
when you're faced with stress and strife.
I will be your wall.

My love will never hurt you...
That is not my intent.
My purpose is to love you.
That is why I was sent.
I will be your wall.

UNTIL THE END OF TIME

Sometimes in life we're unwilling
to say the words that we need to say.
Possessing life is fulfilling,
but sometimes life leads our minds astray.

Your tender touch sends me reeling.
Your laughter can steal my heart away.
Don't want to give up this feeling.
I might as well give my life away.

The thought of living without you
is not one that I could entertain.
I've been searching my whole life through
for someone to love, but all in vain.

Seems that there's nothing I can do
but be yours
until the end
of time.

So now I'm missing you only
the pain of leaving you grows each day.
Never felt so cold and lonely.
Words can't express what I have to say.

I'm needing you just to hold me.
I need to feel your tender embrace.
I need your words to enfold me,
need to lay eyes on your smiling face.

Unending thoughts all about you
but they're all leading me the same way.
I wait in longing without you.
Needing to be with you every day.

Seems that there's nothing I can do
but be yours
until the end
of time.

THE ONE WHO TRULY LOVES YOU

My love's bright enough to destroy the sun

and when every star is dimmed but one

maybe at that time you'll see

that the one who truly loves you is me.

THE ONE THING MISSING

I looked for you,
but you couldn't be found.
Caught in a nightmare,
a world without sound.
Trying to change
all the choices I've made.
Slowly I waken
and slowly you fade.

The one thing missing was you.
One kiss from you and I knew.

Love still eludes
me at every turn.
The flame for you
will eternally burn.
Finding frustration,
caught up in this maze.
Then I looked up
and was lost in your gaze.

The one thing missing was you.
One kiss from you and I knew.

You look right through me
right down to my soul
vulnerable
you have taken control.
Baring the scars of
love's eternal stain.
Trying to change
but myself I remain.

BROKEN WING

The sun has risen high,
dominating the sky and in the center is you,
just you,
only you.

Shining the light of love,
fills my world with its light, but still all I see
is you,
only you.

The light is shining bright
and I long to embrace, but I can't show my face
to you,
only you.

Take these broken wings.
Fix them so I can fly and in the sky we'll meet.
Take these broken wings.
My love for you grows stronger with every heartbeat.

My voice is soft and frail
as it calls in the night, I have so much to say
to you,
only you.

I try to close my eyes,
but I feel you all around, the vision remains
of you,
only you.

I move my broken wing
and I turn to the light, filled with terror and fright
of you,
losing you.

Take these broken wings.
Fix them so I can fly and in the sky we'll meet.
Take these broken wings.
My love for you grows stronger with every heartbeat.

Afraid, I turn away,
though there's a world all around, I hear no other sound,
but you,
only you.

A haunting melody
fills the air all around, echoing its beauty
like you,
just like you.

At night, when I'm alone,
my mind is not free, all that I can see
is you,
only you.

Take these broken wings
Fix them so I can fly and in the sky we'll meet.
Take these broken wings.
My love for your grows stronger with every heartbeat.

LOVE YOU FOR THE REST OF MY LIFE

Don't want you to mistake me
if it seems I'm coming on too strong,
but lately I've
been thinking 'bout the way that we were.

It makes no sense.
It's so intense
and it's only getting stronger.
You're by my side.
The changing tide.
It's a feeling I can't hide
I wanna love you for the rest of my life.

I don't need complications.
I've grown too strong and I've come too far,
but lately I've
been thinking that this isn't a game.

It seems to me
that this won't be
a passing summer romance.
Quarter 'til two.
Thinking of you
and there's nothing I can do
I wanna love you for the rest of my life.

My powers of perception
say be cautious of the words you hear,
but lately I've
been thinking that there's nothing to fear.

We'll take it slow.
In time we'll know
if this love will last forever.
Pray every night
with all my might
and you can make the story right.
I wanna love you for the rest of my life.

SOME PEOPLE

Some people love in a chain reaction.
Some people love just a fraction.
Some people love you in secret.
Some love and forget.

For some people love's a drop in an ocean.
For some it's as vast as an ocean.
For some love's just a lost emotion
For some a discarded notion.

Touch me,
hold me,
show me,
Your love is real.

Some people love you too strong.
Some people won't love you long
Some people get lost in emotions.
Some people go through the motions.

Some people dance around their feelings.
Some so caught up in concealing.
For some people love is a life-quest.
For others a conquest.

Touch me,
hold me,
show me,
Your love is real.

For some people love's a form of possession.
For some people love is confession.
For some people love is a precious jewel.
For some an unbreakable rule.

Now I don't know the whole deal.
I only know how I feel.
I don't claim to have all the answers.
...just take your chances.

IF YOU ARE THE RIVER

If you are the river
I'll be the sea.
Whatever you ask for
That's what I'll be.
Whenever you hunger
I'll be all that you need.

So when confusion's clouding your eyes
seek the love that I can't disguise
and just like an angel
I'll lift you up.

If you are the river
I'll be the sea.
Like flowers to sunlight
bend towards me.
Like a child in the darkness
I'll be the light that you need.

And if you missed the look in my eyes
you'll feel the passion burning deep down inside
reach for me gently
and don't let me go.

If you are the river
I'll be the sea.
When life's overwhelming
breathe deeply of me.
Just let me get closer
and I'll set you free.

So when temptation's starting to rise
and you need freedom just look in my eyes
and I'll still be waiting
until the end of time.

If you are the river
I'll be the sea.

WHEN HE TOUCHES ME

A silent wind,
a gentle rain,
a lover's touch
to ease the pain,
a heart to have,
a hand to hold,
sometimes the world
can feel so cold,

but when he touches me,
he touches all of me,
the power sets me free
and it feels like everything
is gonna be alright.

An eagle cries,
a dove takes flight,
I feel his body
in the night,
he holds me close,
I sleep in peace
and all the fears
inside me cease,

'cause when he touches me,
he touches all of me,
his power sets me free
and it feels like everything
is gonna be alright.

The planets move,
the seasons change,
the stars burn out
and rearrange,
the oceans ebb,
emotions flow,
I don't know much,
but this I know...

that when he touches me,
he touches all of me,
his power sets me free
and it feels like everything
is gonna be alright.

ABOUT THE AUTHOR

Born on March 25th 1975, Kyran Daisy is an Aries true to form. His parents, both being mixed (his mother-Indian and Portuguese; his father-Scottish and Black) and from the West Indies, were careful to raise their children with a strong sense of themselves, focusing on education and raising them without color lines. Kyran attended college at Boston University where he received his BA in psychology in 1997. It was in the fall of 1995, after the passing of his grandmother the preceding spring, that he began writing after hearing Maya Angelou speak in a film during a communications class. The poem inspired was "Can't Nobody Take Me Away!" which was received with an ovation when read publicly at a Black History Month celebration on campus.

The poems poured out in a prolific and honest stream of consciousness. Sometimes writing in spurts that would produce thirty poems in a span of two weeks. Each poem touching on a topic that deeply concerned or inspired him and allowing some deep emotions a creative release. Yearning for new experiences Kyran set his sights on seeing the world.

Through Boston University, he was able to study in London in the spring of 1996 as well as participate in the Semester at Sea Program through the University of Pittsburgh that summer, traveling to Tahiti, Fiji, Western Samoa, Australia, New Zealand, and Hawaii. In the spring of 1997 Kyran embarked on yet another journey with Semester at Sea, where he studied music, acting, and dance. This time traveling to Venezuela, Brazil, Kenya, Tanzania, Vietnam, China, with performances at schools and orphanages in India, the Philippines, South Africa, and Japan. Coming into the world as well as coming out to it added to the stream of changes that characterized this tumultuous period in his life.

Traveling to over thirty countries and having touched life on six continents, the travels as well as his own life experiences and lessons have helped to enrich a fertile imagination and color the content of his poetry with a wide variety of perspectives and topics. After the second voyage, he moved to Los Angeles for a year then returned to New York in the Fall of 1998. Since then he has taken classes in fine art and graphic design as well as jewelry design. Kyran continues to write and is currently working towards a Graduate Gemologist degree at The Gemological Institute of America (GIA).